BUILT TO LAST

BUILT TO LAST

Copyright © 2018 Courtney Richards

Published by Beyond Expectations Media

ISBN 978-1-912845-06-4 (sc)

ISBN 978-1-912845-07-1 (e)

All rights reserved. No part of this publication may be reproduced, stored in a retrieval system, or be transmitted, in any form, or by any means, mechanical, electronic, photocopying or otherwise without prior written consent of the publisher.

Any people depicted in stock imagery provided by iStockphoto and Unsplash, are models and such images are being used for illustrative purposes only.

All Scripture quotations marked (NKJV) are from the New King James Version of the Bible. Copyright © 1979, 1980, 1982 by Thomas Nelson, Inc. Used by permission. All rights reserved.

All Scripture quotations marked (AMP) are from the Amplified Bible. Old Testament copyright © 1965, 1987 by Zondervan Corporation. The Amplified New Testament copyright © 1954, 1958, 1987 by the Lockman Foundation. Used by permission. All rights reserved.

All Scripture quotations marked (ESV) are from The Holy Bible, English Standard Version. Copyright © 2001 by Crossways Bibles. Used by permission. All rights reserved.

All Scripture quotations marked (NLT) are from the Holy Bible, New Living Translation. Copyright © 1996, 2004. Used by permission of Tyndale House Publishers. All rights reserved.

All Scripture quotations marked (EXB) are from The Expanded Bible, Copyright © 2011 Thomas Nelson Inc. All rights reserved.

Welcome!

Thank you for taking this journey today. I pray your investment of time is richly rewarded as you open your mind to wisdom and revelation truth about your relationships.

This program can eliminate years pain, disappointment and wasted experiences.

Life is always teaching us something. The lessons we learn from the situations of life are entirely based on our individual worldview. Do you live in a friendly or hostile universe? Einstein said the answer to this question is the most important decision you'll ever make.

3 Great Laws

- The Law of Entropy
- The Law of Observation
- The Law of the Seed

These 3 laws when combined together create something quite spectacular.

The Law of Entropy creates the understanding that we've been given delegated dominion & authority (Genesis 1:28) and unless we do something positive, nature (default position of chaos & disorder) will take its course. We have to enforce order. According to Psalm 1:1 (AMP), we are blessed when we choose not to be a passive and inactive bystander in the situations of life.

The way in which we see & perceive things (The Law of Observation) determines our emotions, our expectations and what we ultimately do about situations and circumstances around us; and The Law of the Seed teaches us that we have the ability and power to change our future by what we do with the seed in our possession today. We have the ability to root out bad seeds and plant new ones for a desired harvest.

Understanding and making use of this knowledge with fundamentally transform your relationships.

Ready, Steady, **SHIFT**

Please circle the Y = yes or the N = no, in answer to the following questions.

Ready

There is time in my life to invest in my own development	Y or N
A gap exists between where I want to be and where I am right now	Y or N
I can work on tasks that will help me to develop and grow	Y or N

Willing

I am willing to perform whatever is necessary to reach my goal and aims	Y or N
I am willing to SHIFT in my thinking concerning relationships and marriage	Y or N
I am willing to attempt new ways of achieving my goals	Y or N

Able

I have the commitment I need to succeed	Y or N
I have the support I need to make significant changes to my life	Y or N
I am mentally ready for a different approach to my life	Y or N
I am physically prepared for the encounters I may not have experienced before	Y or N

7-10 Y   This program will be effective, exciting and rewarding for you

5-7 Y   You may need to make some adjustments before starting this program

1-5 Y   You are not interested in SHIFTING!

What do you want to get from this program? --

BUILT TO LAST

Use the notes sections in this workbook to make notes whilst the facilitator takes you through the session.

 Did you know that there are around 250,000 marriages in Britain each year costing around £2.5Bn

No-one gets married expecting to get divorced (unless it's a business arrangement). However, at a ratio of nearly 1 in 2 and costing around £40,000 per couple, there are around 115,000 divorces every year.

OUR AIM
Relating—and the quality of our relationships—is of deep, natural, and inherent concern for all of us and like any human endeavour, takes attention, care, and commitment. This program is designed to help you create a SHIFT in your thinking that supports the building of strong relationships allowing you to flourish whether single or married.
For those that are already married, it could serve as a means of identifying where things may have gone wrong and a platform for making things better.

You'll discover a possibility of being related independent of your past, your expectations, your preferences, or your views—a dimension more powerful than personality or circumstance—a dimension where relationships can become an occasion for creativity, vitality, intimacy, and self-expression.

Marriage Beyond Expectations:

- We offer specialist programs covering various aspects of improving relationships.
- We also offer Mediation/ Conflict Resolution service & Relationship Coaching
- Get in touch on 07957125137 or hello@marriagebeyondexpectations.com www.marriagebeyondexpectations.com

Do not be conformed to this world, but be transformed by the renewal of your mind, that by testing you may discern what is the will of God, what is good and acceptable and perfect. Romans 12:2 ESV

Our quest is to wage war on diseased thinking and to embed the divine truth.

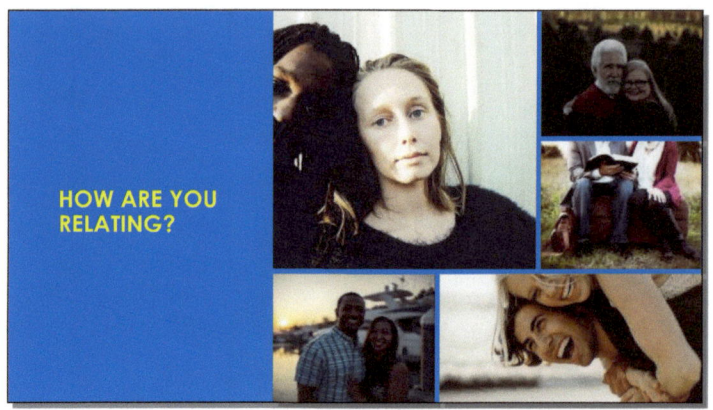

HOW ARE YOU RELATING?

What is the link between your thinking and your relationships?

As a man thinks so is he... Therefore, your relationships resemble your thinking.

Our thoughts lead to actions, and every day this thinking creates a climate that we individually live in.
When we meet someone new, we invite them into our climate. Some seeds will only grow in certain climates – Therefore, we need to be sure to create a climate that the seeds that God has placed in us will grow.

About marriage and other significant relationships, what are your expectations?
Most of us go into relationships on the basis of selfish desires - in other words, *"what do I get out of it..."* Perhaps, you wanted:

- A good cook
- A good lover
- A good looker
- A good cleaner
- A good protector etc.

While useful... all the above are based on what we want to get from the relationship.
Disappointment comes when our pre-set expectations are unfulfilled.

All too often we've pre-rehearsed marriage and our spouse is now failing to meet the picture we've already created.

So, are you marrying a principle or a person?

Today, our focus is on creating a marriage that's designed to last. Everyone has hopes and dreams for a life together that will work, so regarding your hopes and dreams; **what are they built on?** sand or rock?

I want to challenge you to think on things that motivates growth in your relationships.

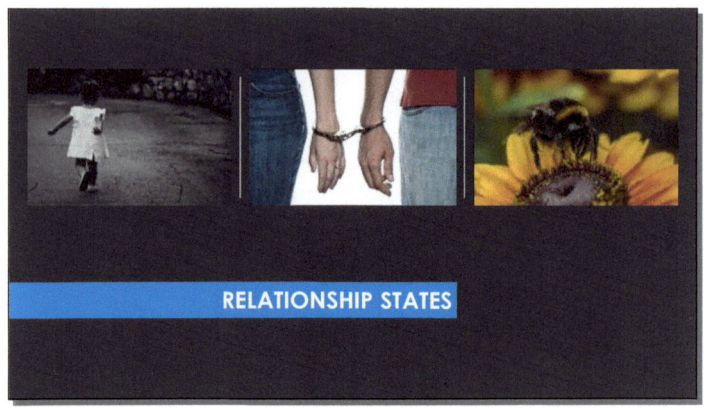

RELATIONSHIP STATES

The word relationship defines the state of our connection to another human being. When we enter a relationship, we bring to the table our ideologies (mindsets).

Independence - A relationship is about sharing life. Therefore, an independent mindset which only considers or relies on self is incompatible with marriage.

Independent minded people want to get married but have not created any room in their lives for another person. They feel they can do it all by themselves and have no real need for another person. When they do get into a relationship, they are focused on what belongs to them (my car, my house, my money etc.).

I'm not saying that you shouldn't have separate accounts etc., what I am saying is the mindset of possessiveness and selfishness is incompatible as a good foundation for a lasting relationship.

Co-dependence - A mindset where you give up your own individuality and identity and organise your life around that of another person making them the centre of your world.

Co-dependence has at its root the notion that someone else (often a spouse or close friend etc.) is more important than you are – placing them at the centre of your world.

Now let's make this clear, esteeming others more highly than ourselves is in fact godly (Philippians 2:3). However, the problems occur when our desire to please others overtakes and overrides the divine order for our lives. In so doing we make the other person more important than our creator – in other words, idolatry.

Dr. Jerry Grillo put it this way, *"If helping you is hurting me, I stop helping you."*

Co-dependence initially appears loving and caring on the outside but closer inspection would reveal that one party has suppressed their divine calling and isn't fully expressed as the person they were intended to be.

Inter-dependence - Interdependence recognises and allows for freedom of choice and expression within a relationship to the benefit or detriment of the parties involved.

Co-dependence is similar in that actions of one affects the other, however co-dependence does not allow the room for individual freedom of choice or expression and thereby being restrictive to one of the participants within the relationship.

Psychotherapist Barton Goldsmith Ph.D. explained interdependence this way:

The healthiest way we can interact with those close to us is by being truly interdependent. This is where two people, both strong individuals, are involved with each other, but without sacrificing themselves or compromising their values. What they have is a balanced relationship, and unfortunately it is not all that common. But it is attainable with just a little awareness and understanding.

Ephesians 4:3–16 explains that we are one body but with individual and distinct callings and that we are at maximum strength when each person understands and flows in their calling. By exalting another's gift and calling to the suppression of our own is ego-based disconnectedness at work.

Considering your relationship mindset:

- ✓ Is it in the right state to thrive?
- ✓ What changes will you need to make to create the right foundation?

List what you'll need to **start, stop or continue**.

PILLARS OF A SUCCESSFUL MARRIAGE

Purpose of relationships and marriage

WHAT
- Humans were created to rule the earth - Delegated authority Genesis 1:26-28 & Psalm 115:16
- Our lives are based solely and entirely on our choices and the totality of creation responds to our choices Duet 30:19
- We have the power of choice to take actions. Not taking action is also a choice.

HOW
- The creator wants us to rule using his system - called the Kingdom of God, where we rule through and by a knowledge of his kingdom. However, he will not violate your choices if you choose something else.
- *...and have put on the new man who is renewed in knowledge according to the image of Him who created him.* Colossians 3:10
- It is therefore important to renew your mind according to his image.
- Thy kingdom come they will be done... The will of the father should be preeminent in all relationships.

> **Question to self...** What is the purpose for this connection?

The global purpose for Adam and Eve, was that together they will rule the earth.

The most important facet for any relationship is the presence of love. Not the butterflies in your stomach kind of love, but the love that's based on a decision to give to another person at the expense of yourself - without the guarantee of getting anything back.

reating firm foundations based on understanding will support a long-term relationship. Let's address some of the thinking errors that cause poor foundations.

- **Women trying to make the man better** - many women invest a lot of time, energy and resources in a relationship trying to make a man decent to marry – **WRONG!**
  Trying to change him so that he fits your needs is (a) selfish in that the underpinning motive is self-serving and, (b) futile as it will not create lasting change unless he is powering the change process himself.
  What am I not saying? I'm not saying you shouldn't support him, I'm saying you should do it on the basis that he wants change for himself.
  I've observed women whose relationship actions with their men resemble a person pushing a stubborn mule up a hill. He's totally disengaged and only doing it under duress. **Save yourself the waste of energy, and this foundation is incapable to standing the test of time.**

- **Men don't expect your wife to take the place of your mother**, she's also not your maid or cleaner. It's not her responsibility to pay for your life etc.
  I've observed some men go into a relationship with the express view that their wife is there to look after them becoming angry and frustrated when this doesn't happen according to their expectations.
  I've observed some men act as spoilt teenagers with their feet up at home doing nothing until their wife has got home from work to cook for them. I'm not saying that your wife shouldn't cook or clean etc., what I am saying is the expectation as a precondition **is a foundation that will only support failure.**

- **Contrary to popular opinion, it is the man's job to nourish and cherish his woman, not the other way around.** Ephesians 5:25-29
  In truth we are to nourish and cherish each other. However, the man is the instigator of the process. The man sows the seed of love in demonstrating to his wife that she is precious. The wife then reciprocates based on the love that she's been shown.
  Building a relationship where the nourishing and cherishing is initiated by the woman will always be on a shaky foundation that will lead to under-appreciation and burnout.

- Women may be called the weaker vessel, but they are not less than…
  It is important to recognise that women are seen by God no differently to how he sees men – we are equal under God. God made a woman to be the weaker vessel not to be put down but because she has a different (not a lesser) function.
  There is neither Jew nor Greek, there is neither slave nor free, there is neither male nor female; for you are all one in Christ Jesus. Galatians 3:28 (NKJV)
  Building a relationship where the man thinks he's greater than his wife, or a wife thinking she is less than her husband denies divine order and creates an unstable foundation.

- **Being saved doesn't automatically make your relationship work.** God will not take away your choices and the resulting consequences thereof. *Likewise, husbands, live with your wives in an understanding way* - 1 Peter 3:7a. Are you saying I need to understand my wife - **YES!**
  God puts the onus on the man to work to understand how his wife ticks. She's not a man and is wired differently. Seeking to appreciate her difference will also cause your prayers not to be hindered! **Christian or not, failing to appreciate your respective differences demonstrates a lack of foresight in the construction of a long-term relationship.**

- **Men, it's okay for your wife to have a different opinion to yours** – having a different opinion isn't an attack on your manliness…
  It's important to recognise that Adam needed help, hence God created Eve. Help by its very nature brings a different opinion/perspective for it to be helpful.
  Being open to this input demonstrates your humility and recognition of the benefits of synergy. **Not recognising this fact and allowing your ego to get in the way of finding better solutions is a sure way to create a poor foundation for marriage.**

Are you SHIFTING?

For example, I thought……. (old beliefs, I now reject), today I'm moving towards (new beliefs)…

List the ways below:

> **FOUNDATION OF UNDERSTANDING**
>
> **Myths:**
>
> - **We all tend to believe that others see the world as we do**
> - **We believe that everyone views us the same way we see ourselves**
> - **Leads to mismatched/ unmet needs**

We all tend to believe that others see the world as we do.

We believe that everyone views us the same way we see ourselves.

This leads to mismatched/ unmet needs

Question: Does 1+1=2 all the time?

What's the impact on my relationships when:
- I don't appreciate my spouse/ partner's point of view?
- I judge them based on my own fixed frame of reference?

As well as being a story about pride - The Tower of Babel project failed because of a lack of communication.

Two cannot walk together unless they agree Amos 3:3

The effectiveness of communication is governed by many factors
✓ Age
✓ Education
✓ Values
✓ Past experience etc.

People don't hear what you're saying they interpret what you say... It is therefore essential to check understanding to build a foundation of trust and co-operation, so you are both singing from the same hymn sheet.

- ✓ What areas of my relationship are showing signs of poor communication?
- ✓ What can you do to seek understanding?

List what you'll need to **start, stop or continue**.

INTEGRITY

The qualification of being honest and having strong moral principles; adherence to moral uprightness. It is generally a personal choice to hold oneself to consistent moral and ethical standards.

- It is simply being truthful, honest and straight! The fact is that in our complicated world, this isn't always so easy…
- A lack of it will be corrosive to your foundations quicker than almost anything else…
- Your integrity is inextricably linked to your value system which have been shaped by your experiences, upbringing and education etc. and is potentially different for each person.
- For consistency, it is therefore important to choose God's standards of measure.

Where do you stand on key issues? For example, what does honesty mean to you? Your views might be different…

Are your public and private actions consistent? Some relationships are characterised by being what seems like a public success, but in reality, are private failures.

How open are you about where you are now? Being clear with the difference between where you are now vs. where you want to be (aspirations). For example, wanting to be a person that's diligent and being such are two different things.

Relationships are often corrupted by misaligned standards and expectations. For example, each of you might have a different interpretation of what the term *'being on time'* means. Turning up at 10:30 for a 10 am meeting might be considered on time by one and not by the other.

Integrity is fundamentally the standards to which you hold yourself accountable. What you do in private when do one else is watching. Integrity in critically important for the health of your relationship as it is the supports the building of trust.

Do you mean what you say? Or do you say one thing and do another?

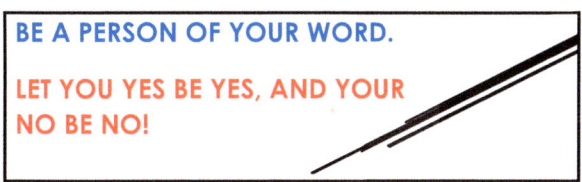

BE A PERSON OF YOUR WORD.

LET YOU YES BE YES, AND YOUR NO BE NO!

What actions can I take to build integrity into my life as an individual?

What standards can we agree to work to as a couple?

Consider and discuss any changes needed.

RESPECT
A feeling of deep admiration for someone based on their abilities, qualities, or achievements.
Due regard for the feelings, wishes, or rights of others.

Mutual respect is one of the cornerstones of all successful relationships. Without mutual respect couples are unlikely to be able to solve problems. The loss of mutual respect can destroy a marriage quickly, or more often, lead to a painful, stressful and unhappy life for a couple.

Because it is linked to the feeling of deep admiration for someone based on their abilities, qualities, or achievements and due regard for the feelings, wishes, or rights of others - the scriptures encourage us think on good things...

The biggest proof of love is the desire to give

Husbands love your wives	Wives respect your husbands
Husbands love your wife relates to sacrificial giving (time, resources, position etc) based on unqualified acceptance – irrespective of performance. Being loved motivates the women to respect.	Wives respect your husband's relates to giving honour and esteem irrespective of performance. Being respected energises/ motivates men to love.

Both are different aspects of giving that's difficult to give at times but starts from the foundation of service one to another.

What can I do to establish & show respect to my spouse?

- Being consistent in considering and valuing your spouse
- Active Listening
- Avoid treating each other in rude and disrespectful ways, e.g., you do not engage in name calling, and do not insult or demean your spouse or partner

Managing the elephants while the ants walk by...
This term relates the small (often unconscious) actions that show disrespect (micro inequities). Individually don't cause a relationship to fail but the cumulative effect over time will erode the foundations of any relationship.

Examples of micro inequities
1. Not allowing them to finish their sentence
2. Ignoring
3. Tutting or rolling your eyes when they speak
4. Not acknowledging their opinion

> In what small ways have I been showing disrespect?
>
> In what small ways can you show that you affirm your spouse?

Micro-affirmations are the small actions that communicate value and respect to another.

Examples of micro-affirmations
1. Asking for their opinion
2. Acknowledging their presence
3. Attributing & Giving credit
4. Smiling

Regarding respecting each other, consider the following:

- *But now you yourselves are to put off all these: anger, wrath, malice, blasphemy, filthy language out of your mouth. Do not lie to one another, since you have put off the old man with his deeds* **Colossians 3:8-9**
- *Let no corrupt word proceed out of your mouth, but what is good for necessary edification, that it may impart grace to the hearers.* **Ephesians 4:29**
- *A good man out of the good treasure of his heart brings forth good; and an evil man out of the evil treasure of his heart[a] brings forth evil. For out of the abundance of the heart his mouth speaks.* **Luke 6:45**

Remember, communication is about what you say both verbally and non-verbally.

ENDURANCE
The ability to endure an unpleasant or difficult process or situation without giving way, and the ability to withstand wear and tear.

Endurance, in my opinion, is much more powerful than commitment alone. If we are to lay claim to a successful marriage, we simply must stick with it no matter what! Remember, marriage is ordained of God and is a covenant.

With the exception of any type of abuse in a marriage, your marriage is worth your best efforts. Time and time again, it is not uncommon to hear a person that has opted for a divorce, to later in their life make a comment suggesting, perhaps, that they probably could have worked things out, or that they wish they had never opted for divorce. Considering the pathetic statistics for successful second marriages, working through the rough times of your first marriage is most likely worth it for everyone involved.

Instead of cussing them…
Instead of bailing out (emotionally or physically), hang on in there…
The prize awaits those that hang in there and **work to make things better…**

Quitting happens in the mind before it physically manifests.

What changes in thinking will you need to make that will support endurance?

List them.

FORGIVENESS

Like respect - forgiveness is another aspect of love (decision-based giving).

Especially when the Word tells us that we all stumble and sin in many ways - forgiveness is something that we all had better learn to get good at - and that includes you!

Holding to unforgiveness is like drinking poison and hoping that the other person dies... As you are one flesh with your spouse, unforgiveness poisons the entire relationship.

With that said, **can you afford to not give this precious gift?**
God doesn't ask you to give something that you don't already have. He gave you forgiveness by sending his son to die in your place and, therefore expects you to do the same – **especially to your spouse.**

While we're on the subject... the word *offended* in Matthew 24:10-12 is the Greek word *skándalon* – meaning, the trigger of a trap (the mechanism closing a trap down on the unsuspecting victim); (figuratively) an *offense*, putting a *negative cause-and-effect relationship* into motion.

Also, ("the means of stumbling") stresses the *method* (*means*) of *entrapment*, i.e. how someone is caught by *their own devices* (like their personal bias, carnal thinking).

Unforgiveness is therefore a personal trap waiting to hook you.

Are you offended?
Let it go - release yourself.

FORGIVENESS:

If not now, when?

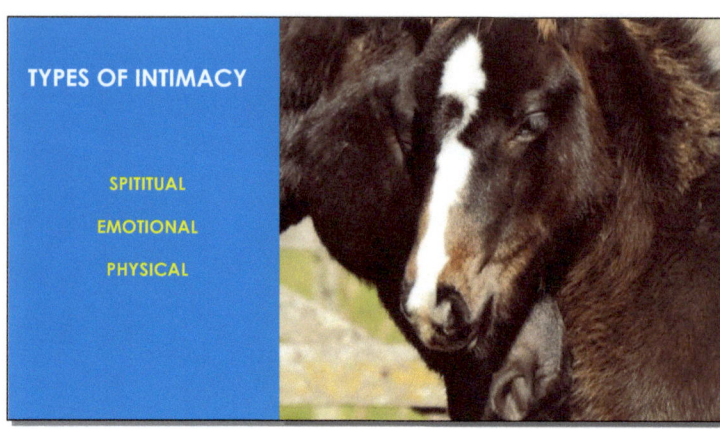

In God's sexual economy intimacy is 3-dimensional. Ephesians 5:32 tells us *"and they shall become one flesh...this is a profound mystery..."*. The Apostle Paul was referring to couples coming together in a marital relationship. It is important to note that it is not a mystery to connect physically. Anyone can do that...even the beasts of the fields can mate! However, it is a profound mystery to connect with our bodies, our souls, and our spirits. When God created male and female and brought them together as husbands and wives, He had more planned for this union than just procreation. God desired that His creation experience the profound mystery of becoming one at every level of their relationship. God desired for His creation to enjoy *"total intimacy"*.

Leave and cleave
You can only be one flesh when you leave what you've been previously attached to... and cleave to your spouse.

- Be it your parents or a previous spouse/ partner.
- Intimacy can only thrive where there are places of exclusivity reserved just for the two of you (spiritually, emotionally & physically).
- It is important to define it and maintain boundaries of what belongs only to the two of you.

..."and they were naked and unashamed" Gen. 2:24
Intimacy thrives when we have nothing to hide and there is total acceptance and valuing of the other person.

Spiritual Intimacy
Spiritual intimacy is a sense of unity and mutual commitment to God's purpose for your lives and marriage, along with a respect for the special dreams of each other's hearts. It's the greatest depth of intimacy we experience in marriage. A godly marriage happens when two people

who are created in God's image join together to help each other fulfil God's calls on their lives.

- When you value each other spiritually, you partner with God to help your spouse reach their spiritual potential.
- This means being committed to pursuing God as individuals, and together as a couple - by putting in the spiritual work. Praying together and inviting God into your circumstances.
- Few things are more powerful than a man and woman praying for their children, their jobs, their finances, and their lives together. Apply enthusiasm to your spiritual life. Pray together, worship together, and seek God together.

> **What small changes will you agree to make?**

Emotional intimacy

Emotional intimacy occurs when there is enough trust and communication between you and your spouse that it allows you both to share your innermost selves. Deep emotional intimacy is when we feel wholly accepted, respected, and admired in the eyes of our mate even when they know our innermost struggles and failures. Emotional intimacy fosters compassion and support, providing a firm foundation for a marriage to last a lifetime.

Why is it hard to develop emotional intimacy?

1. Fear of rejection. (If I share the essence of who I really am, you might criticise or reject the real me.)
2. Unfamiliarity with our own feelings, needs, or wants. (If I'm not sure what I feel or need, how can I share it with you?)
3. Lack of vocabulary to communicate our feelings accurately or to verbalise exactly what we want or need. (If I don't know the words to describe what I'm feeling or needing, then it's easier to just keep my thoughts to myself.)
4. Expecting our spouse to just know. (You can read my mind, can't you?)

REMEMBER ITS ALL ABOUT THE INNER GAME OF THE HEART

Emotional intimacy TO DO List:

- Pay attention to your own emotions.
- Become familiar with your "inner self."
- Evaluate your past.
- Determine to be a "safe" person for your spouse to share his/her emotions.
- Deal with conflict swiftly

Physical intimacy is like unto nothing else - in that you have a need that can only be fulfilled by the other person. This puts you in a position of weakness, and the other in a position of strength (and vice versa).

This strength could be abused by shutting down and using your body as a weapon. However, when we learn that our bodies no longer belong to us, we approach physical intimacy with the attitude of service - giving.

Warning signs
- You find it easier to talk about personally sensitive aspects of your life to others.
- When you have important news and you don't share it first with your spouse.
- You feel unable to show your feelings to your spouse (love, happiness, sadness, frustration, excitement).
- You feel unable to discuss the lack of intimacy.
- You don't think lack of emotional intimacy is a problem.

What steps will you take to make a meaningful difference?

5 MUST HAVE'S
- Trust
- Conflict
- Commitment
- Accountability
- Focus on results

In some ways, marriage can be likened to a team in an organisation.

- What is the purpose of your team?

A team vision is what keeps people together when things get tough.

Clarity of purpose is what generates energy, excitement and hope (working towards a better future).

- Know your lane
- Train your giftings

Focus on your individual purpose within your team's overall plan.
Why settle for mediocre, develop you giftings to its highest possible elevation - this adds value to the team.

All great teams (including married teams) display the following must haves:

1. **Trust** – Not to be confused a trust built on knowing what someone will do next (predictive trust), for example predicting that your spouse will be do something based on what they've done in the past; but a trust underpinned by the ability to be transparent and vulnerable with each other. This is demonstrated by the ability to admit an error, to be open about personal struggles and secrets, to be open to listen to your spouse's views.

   Predictive trust is also important and is comprised of:
   Capability – your ability to do something
   Consistency – your ability to produce results over time
   Commitment – your ability to be deeply engaged in the relationship or course of action.

2. **Conflict** - not to be confused with mean spirited conflict, but healthy and passionate expressions based on what's important. This causes creative solutions to be birthed. *Iron sharpens iron as a man sharpens the countenance of his friend* Proverbs 27:17
For a team to grow there has to be healthy challenge. Once trust is in place a stability is created that enables passionate discourse, leading to growth.

3. **Commitment** - the decision to stay the course and work problems out.
We often conduct our relationships no different to what happens on social media where, when problems occur the solution is to unfriend them. The marriage vows say, *for better or worse...* pointing to the committed and permanent nature of the union. A decision to stand by each other not just in the good times but also in the bad. *"The ultimate measure of a man is not where he stands in moments of comfort and convenience, but where he stands at times of challenge and controversy."* Martin Luther King

4. **Accountability** - based on the team purpose and the understanding of interdependence - it is the holding each other accountable and supporting where necessary to deliver for the team goals.
One of the hallmarks of a great relationship or team is the ability to challenge each other to give their best. Sometimes this challenge is demonstrated by a *'kick up the butt'* to get back in-line. We all have the potential of straying off course from time to time and need a critical friend to give us needed feedback.

5. **Focus on results** - having clarity of where you are both going and what you are working to achieve, keeping your eyes on the prize and not getting distracted.
Many teams and relationships have had to go through times of restructuring when they've found that they've lost their focus and have become less effective.
Being clear on where you're both going is important as is keeping the main thing the main thing.

What areas of the *must have's* are you committing to work on over the next 30 days?

KEY MESSAGES

- Your mindset will create the conditions for growth or demise or your relationship.
- Your actions towards your spouse are a picture of your heart condition.
- Develop total intimacy (spiritual, emotional & physical).
- Know the divine purpose for your union and work towards it.
- It takes work!

- ✓ Your mindset will create the conditions for growth or demise or your relationship.
- ✓ Your actions towards your spouse are a picture of your heart condition.
- ✓ Develop total intimacy (spiritual, emotional & physical).
- ✓ Know the divine purpose for your union and work towards it.
- ✓ It takes work!

> Own your own happiness
> Challenge your story
> Enjoy the journey not the destination
> Make your relationship count
> Work to make things better

What questions do I have?

NOTES

NOTES

Also available from Beyond Expectations Media

Built To Last

Making Difference Work

Chaos To Order

Through The Storm

Untying Fear Knots

Eye 2 Eye

    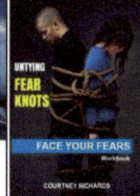 

GYMNASIUM
OF THE MIND